Autoimmune Cookbook:

Delicious Autoimmune Protocol Paleo Diet Recipes For Naturally Healing Autoimmune Disease and Disorders

By

Valerie Alston

Table of Contents

Introduction 5

1. Soups 8
2. Appetizer/ Snacks 12
3. Beverages 17
4. Salads 21
5. Breakfast Recipes 24
6. Beef Recipes 29
7. Desert Recipes 36

Final Words 38

Thank You Page 40

Autoimmune Cookbook: Delicious Autoimmune Protocol Paleo Diet Recipes For Naturally Healing Autoimmune Disease and Disorders

By Valerie Alston

© Copyright 2014 Valerie Alston

Reproduction or translation of any part of this work beyond that permitted by section 107 or 108 of the 1976 United States Copyright Act without permission of the copyright owner is unlawful. Requests for permission or further information should be addressed to the author.

This publication is designed to provide accurate and authoritative information in regard to the subject matter covered. This work is sold with the understanding that the publisher is not engaged in rendering legal, accounting, or other professional services. If legal advice or other expert assistance is required, the services of a competent professional person should be sought.

First Published, 2014

Printed in the United States of America

Introduction

The Autoimmune Paleo Diet has grown into popularity over the past several years and it certainly cultivated a lot of members or followers of this kind of diet. The idea of this type of diet is to only consume foods that were present during the Paleolithic period like the fruits, vegetables, plants and even meat that were consumed by the people in that time.

Over the years, people have developed their own versions of the Paleo diet. They have their own recipes and approaches in eating foods like our Paleolithic ancestors did and these versions have been effective for them and for other people who have tried them. This is true because they stick to the number one rule of the Paleo diet, that is to only consume foods that have naturally grown in our environment without any preservatives and where no food processing were used.

Autoimmune Paleo Diet targets the autoimmune system specifically using the right kind of food intake and having the right amount of food taken in the body to boost the immune system and help in the fight of autoimmune diseases.

Autoimmune disease is a condition where the body can no longer distinguish healthy cells from bad bacteria or bad cells causing the immune system to attack not only the bad cells but also the good ones. This self-tissue attacking disease has plagued many individuals for a very long time and is still a cause of death in all countries in the world. It highly depends on what we consume and our diet primarily. Keep in mind that there are many autoimmune diseases that have come forward and attacked individuals and right now, the count is at 80 types with more and more rearing their heads as newly developed autoimmune diseases. So to fight the good fight, the Autoimmune Paleo Diet program was launched not only by one person or one company, but a bunch of other individuals who want to keep themselves and others healthy and to prolong human life. Thus, recipes of different Autoimmune Paleo diets have emerged to guide people into eating healthy and life-saving foods.

Just to give you a snapshot of what and what not to eat when in a Paleo diet:

What is good to eat?

Vegetables, Fruits, Seafood, Lean Meats, Healthy Fats, Nuts & Seeds

What to avoid?

Processed Food and Sugars, Grains, Dairy, Starches, Legumes, Alcohol

1. Soups

Bone-Broth Stew

Bone broth is good for the Autoimmune system because it is a great source of calcium, magnesium and other nutrients the gut needs to heal. This soup is great to consume in the morning because it will get you started for the day.

What you need:

Pressure cooker, bay leaf, apple cider vinegar (to draw the minerals form the bones), salt to taste(optional), Bones from healthy animals, you can get this at your local butcher for a bulk price, preferably the beef knuckle bones but any other bone will do just fine.

Steps:

Put the bones in the water-filled pressure cooker. Any kind of bone will do, don't worry if they come from different kinds of animals, they can be mixed. Sometimes, some bones do not dissolve or are still perfectly good for another batch of this broth, so put those in a plastic bag and store in the refrigerator.

Add a bay leaf and pour in apple cider vinegar, just a splash. Do not add salt if you will partner your broth with a salty dish. Too much saltiness will just ruin the taste.

For a good gel-like consistency in your broth, use as much bones as you can. You can combine beef, chicken, and pork bones if you like. It just adds variety to the flavor and the less water you use in the broth, the stronger the broth will be in its taste.

Let the broth cook at high pressure for three hours using your pressure cooker. Once done, let it depressurize naturally. Strain the liquid form the bones. You can save the ones that are still intact and just throw away ones that have melted into mush.

Serve hot and enjoy!

Store the excess broth in mason jars and put in the refrigerator for future use. This batch will be good for a week or two when kept in the fridge. You can also put it in the freezer for longer shelf life. Make sure you do not freeze them too much that the jars might break.

Bacon with Asparagus Soup

What you need:

1 bunch of asparagus

5 slices of bacon

1 medium onion (heaping cup)

3 cups bone broth, you can add more or less depending on how you like your soup's consistency

3 tablespoons of olive oil

Salt to taste

Steps:

Clean the asparagus and cut off the bottom about 2-3 inches down and throw away the cut part. The upper parts of the asparagus are softer and much better to eat.

Remove the onion skin and roughly chop it up. You can also mince it you prefer.

Cut the bacon strips into 2-inch sized pieces. This will make it easier to eat and chew.

Put the onions, asparagus, cut bacon, and stock to the pressure cooker and bring to full pressure for 10 minutes. You can also use a stove top in place of the pressure cooker and cook the ingredients on medium heat for 40 minutes.

After the pressure time has elapsed, release the pressure and put the contents into a blender.

Add olive oil and put the lid on and use a dish towel to make sure the hot liquid will not splash on to you. Start the blender on the slowest speed.

Then you should blend on high speed for two minutes, add salt to taste.

Serve hot or you can cook more on simmer.

2. Appetizer/ Snacks

Sweet Potato Fries topped with Garlic Mayo

This sumptuous snack will surely get you stated with your appetite so go ahead and look at how easy it is to make one of these.

What you need:

For the Mayo mixture:

1/2 cup slightly warmed coconut concentrate

1/2 cup warm filtered water

1/4 cup extra-virgin olive oil

3-4 cloves garlic

1/4 teaspoon salt

For the Fries:

3 large sweet potatoes that are peeled and cut into thick fries

4 tablespoons melted solid cooking fat

Sea salt to taste

Steps:

For the mayo, mix the coconut concentrate, olive oil, warm water, garlic cloves, and salt in a blender. Blend high until the sauce thickens which is about a minute or two. Set to cool for 1 hour or alternately putting it in the fridge for 20 minutes. For cold dishes, you can add a little amount of water to dissolve the sauce a bit.

For the fries, preheat the oven at 400 degrees, put the sweet potato fries in a clean container and mix or coat with the cooking fat and sea salt. Place baking sheets with adequate space between them so they can come out crispy, add the sea salt and back for 10-15 minutes. Check the fries, flip them and put them back in the oven. Cook for another 10-15 minutes. Make sure you monitor them so they won't burn.

Mix the mayo into the fries or separately.

Zucchini Cheese Snacks

These healthy tidbits are dairy-free and very nutritious. Zucchini helps in water retention; it improves circulation and a great course of vitamin C. The ingredients are tasty and healthy at the same time. You can serve this to you friends or family in just a few steps:

What you need:

3/4 cup carrot of about 1 medium carrot, finely diced (carrot is used for cheddar color)

3 cup of peeled and sliced zucchini or summer squash, about 2 medium zucchini

¾ cup water (for steaming and to drain afterwards)

4 tablespoons coconut oil, extra virgin olive oil, red palm oil, or cultured ghee

3 – 4 tablespoons nutritional yeast, optional

3 – 4 teaspoons lemon juice or apple cider vinegar

1 – 1 ½ sea salt, or to taste

7 – 8 tablespoons Great Lakes gelatin

1 probiotic capsule (optional)

Steps:

Place your zucchini cheese pan with a non-bleached parchment paper.

Boil water in a small saucepan, add your carrot and peeled zucchini, cover and simmer on medium low heat for about 5-8 minutes.

Drain water completely and save the excess water for cooking the vegetables.

Mix the ingredients in the blender like vegetables, olive oil, and lemon juice or apple cider vinegar. You can also add nutritional yeast or sea salt. Blend on high speed. If extra virgin olive oil is used, wait until the mixture has cooled before adding.

Sprinkle gelatin into the mixture while it is on low speed. Blend high for another few minutes or until mixture is smooth.

You can add probiotics to the mixture but take care not to put it while still hot, wait for the mixture to cool then you can put the probiotics in.

Pour the mixture onto the parchment paper lined pan and keep in the refrigerator overnight. If it cannot be left overnight, wait for at least 3 hours for the mixture to set and if you need a quicker time, put it in the freezer for an hour.

Now you can cut it into squares, slice them or grate them, depends on you. You can use it with other snacks like veggies or salads and out them on snack plates.

Wrap and keep it in the refrigerator or put them on airtight containers. Consume within 10 days for best flavor.

3. Beverages

Turmeric Tea with Anti-Inflammatory benefits

This concoction, from the name itself, is packed with many minerals and nutrients badly needed by the body. A word of caution in making this tea, turmeric is stains like crazy so make sure you use dark clothes in making this. And if your autoimmune disease if Th2, be careful with this one and consult first a doctor.

What you need:

½ Tbsp turmeric powder

32 oz boiling water

1 Tbsp thinly sliced fresh ginger

1 chopped handful cilantro

1 peeled and crushed garlic clove

1 Tbsp olive oil

5 peppercorns, whole

2 lemons, juiced

1 orange, juiced or you can use 1½ tbsp honey

Steps:

Place water and boil on top of the stove. Combine all the ingredients onto a strainer or a teapot then remove the water once boiled and pour it into the pot.

Let it stay for 10 minutes and pour yourself some tea.

Collagen with Berry Smoothie

Another fun and healthy drink for your tummy. It is very easy to prepare and much easier to drink. You can combine this smoothie with some green vegetables that are antioxidants.

What you need:

A banana

¼ cup of water

½ cup of frozen berries

A tablespoon of coconut concentrate

1 tablespoon collagen

1 cup of spinach

Ice cubes if preferred

Steps:

Mix all ingredients into a blender and blend until smooth. You can add ice cubes to make your smoothie cold and thicker in consistency.

Classic Creamy Coconut Milk

A coconut is s good source of vitamins and various minerals. It contains lots of fiber and nutrients for the body. So give this one a try and you will love this guaranteed!

What you need:

2 cups of boiling water

1 cup unsweetened coconut flakes

Sea salt to taste

Steps:

Mix the shredded coconut and the 2 cups of water into the blender and blend in high speed for a few minutes.

Let it cool for about 15 minutes and strain the coconut residue.

Serve immediately.

4. Salads

Asparagus Ribboned Salad

This is a quick and simple way of preparing your vegetables for the night.

What you need:

1-2 pounds asparagus with the white ends trimmed

1 large fennel bulb

¼ cup extra-virgin olive oil

1 juiced lemon

¼ teaspoon lemon zest

¼ teaspoon sea salt

Steps:

Use a vegetable peeler to carve out long stems of the asparagus and place them in a container. The core in the middle, after you have stripped the thin stems, can be discarded or chopped and be added to the salad.

Slice the fennel bulb with a mandolin slicer and place them in a saucer of container.

Add the lemon juice, olive oil, zest and sea salt to taste to the asparagus and fennel.

Then toss to mix.

Tuna Salad Boats

This is a creative and yummy salad and snack for everybody. It incorporates art and food in this quick and easy salad with a dash of extra flavor and sweet texture.

What you need:

2 5oz BPA-free cans of tuna which is already drained

1 small green apple that is cored and finely chopped

1 finely chopped/ minced carrot

2 ribs of finely chopped celery

½ finely chopped cucumber

2 tablespoons of finely chopped red onion

1 clove of minced garlic

1 tablespoon fresh dill

½ cup olive oil

½ lemon, juiced

1 tablespoon apple cider vinegar

½ teaspoon sea salt

2 endive heads

Steps:

Mix the tuna, carrot, apple, onion, celery, dill, and garlic in a large container. Stir in to combine and mix the ingredients and breaking up the clumps of tuna.

Mix the olive oil with the lemon, apple cider vinegar, and sea salt. Stir well until the tuna has absorbed all the oil.

Cut the edges of the endive and separate the leaves.

Put a serving of tune on each leaf and serve

5. Breakfast Recipes

Italian Spicy Sausages

These sausages are great for your everyday snack that you can take anywhere and share with anyone. Take these simple and easy steps in making this wonderful tummy filler.

What you need:

A pound of grass-fed ground beef

A pound of pastured ground pork

A tablespoon of minced fresh oregano

A tablespoon of minced fresh thyme

A tablespoon of minced fresh parsley (optional)

½ teaspoon of sea salt

½ teaspoon of garlic powder

1 tablespoon solid cooking fat

Steps:

Mix the ingredients: pork, ground beef, garlic powder, herbs and salt, in a large bowl and mix in well using your hands. Then form these into 8-10 patties and just place on a plate.

On medium heat, melt the solid cooking fat in the bottom of a cast-iron skillet or frying pan. When the fat is melted and the pan is hot, add the patties and cook 10 minutes per side, or until thoroughly cooked or a bit brown. You may have to do this in two batches or more depends on you. Alternately, you can bake them at 400 degrees for 20 minutes or until they are cooked throughout.

Blueberry Maple Breakfast Sausages

Another kind of sausage for breakfast which will give you the energy you need to take on the day.

What you need:

1 pound of ground pork, pasture

3 tablespoons of maple syrup

Salt

½ cup of fresh berries

1 tablespoon of cultured ghee, bacon fat or coconut oil

Steps:

Combine the ingredients, salt, pork and maple syrup in a bowl and add blueberries then mix again. Form the patties into 3-inch sizes.

Heat the ghee, coconut oil or bacon fat on high heat using a cast iron skillet. Add the sausage patties into the saucepan. Let it cook for about two minutes then turn down the heat to medium-low. Put the cover on top for about six minutes.

Put heat back to medium high and turn sausages over and continue cooking it for 2 minutes.

Lower the heat again, cover with the lid and cook for another 6 minutes.

Once they are brownish and tender, remove from heat and put on a plate.

Serve immediately.

A DIY Skillet Meal

This skillet meal is basically any vegetable you see in your fridge combined with saturated fat, some flavorings and greens and you're good to go. It is easy because you don't need to go out and shop for the ingredients. It is economical, you just need to raid your refrigerator and see what's left inside to cook.

Basically there are 4 things you need for this DIY skillet:

Your preferred saturated fat

Any starchy vegetable left in the fridge

Some flavorings

Green vegetables

Any leftover protein

What you need:

Coconut oil/lard/bacon/duck fat

You choice of yam, sweet potato, winter squash, or carrot

Some flavorings like ginger, garlic, onions, rosemary, shallots, sage, thyme, or cinnamon

One or two vegetables such as cauliflower, broccoli, green beans, zucchini, and mushrooms

Some greens you can add on like chard, kale, spinach or collard greens

Leftover protein like chicken or duck (shredded), ground beef or shredded beef, salmon or bacon

Steps:

Heat the pan with the saturated fat.

Toss in the vegetables and cook for about 15 minutes.

Add some flavorings to the food and add any other vegetable that can be cooked until soft.

Add some greens and the leftover protein on the last few minutes of cooking.

6. Beef Recipes

Even in the Paleo diet, you still need to get some lean meat into your body so beef, pork and chicken are allowed for this diet. So for those who cannot give up their meat or protein sources, this is good news for you.

Here are some beef recipes that are very easy to prepare with lots of nutritional value.

Braised Beef Shanks

What you need:

2-4 pieces of beef shanks

8 cloves of chopped garlic

Sea salt to taste

1 cup of bone broth

2 tablespoons fresh thyme plus a few extra sprigs

½ cup of water

2 tablespoons of coconut oil

Steps:

Your oven must be preheated at 350 degrees and clean the beef shanks while waiting. Pat them thoroughly with salt on both sides to taste.

Heat the coconut oil on a skillet on a medium-high heat. After that sear the shanks for a few minutes per side and add coconut oil if needed. Place the seared shanks in a baking dish.

Turn down the heat of the gas on the skillet to medium from high and sauté the garlic and thyme. Sautee until lightly brown and when it emits a good smell then add the bone broth and water to the skillet. Boil so water can be reduced.

Mix the broth mixture with the shanks and add the remaining thyme sprigs. Then cover them with aluminum foil for 2 hours. Wait until soft and fork-tender.

Indonesian Beef Curry

This is a great recipe for all member of the family that will guarantee satisfied and full tummies.

What you need:

½ cup of unsweetened coconut flakes

1 bunch of separated cilantro, stalks and leaves

1 onion and cut them into quarters

6 cloves of peeled garlic

1 lime, zested and juice reserved

2 inch piece of peeled ginger

2 tablespoons coconut oil

1 cinnamon stick

6 kaffir lime leaves

1 teaspoon turmeric

1 cup bone broth

1 teaspoon sea salt

2 tablespoons of coconut aminos (optional)

2 pounds of beef stew meat

1 head cauliflower, which is processed into "rice" using a food processor

½ cup coconut concentrate

Steps:

Toast the coconut flakes carefully in a skillet over low heat. Stir until light brown and gives off aroma. Transfer the food into a food processor with the cilantro stalks, garlic, onion, ginger, and lime zest and process until a thick paste forms.

Melt the one tablespoon of the coconut oil using heat in the bottom of a heavy-bottomed pot and add the coconut mixture. Cook for 5-10 minutes or until mixture is sticky.

Mix in the other ingredients like the cinnamon stick, turmeric, kaffir lime leaves, sea salt, bone broth, coconut concentrate and stew meat.

Cook the food and cover it and simmer for 90 minutes until the beef is very tender to the touch.

While the beef is being cooked, cook the cauliflower "rice" in the coconut oil until cooked in about ten minutes.

When the curry is cooked, mix in the lime, cilantro leaves and coconut aminos and stir until all are nicely mixed.

Serve the meal on top of the cauliflower "rice".

Autoimmune Protocol Meatloaf

What you need:

1 tablespoon of coconut oil

1 cup cauliflower, which is processed into "rice" using food processor

½ minced onion

1 carrot (peeled and grated)

1 zucchini (peeled and grated)

4 minced cloves garlic

½ cup chopped parsley

2 teaspoons sea salt

2 egg yolks (don't include if you are on the elimination diet)

2 tablespoons fresh thyme and/or marjoram

2 lbs ground beef, pork or lamb mixture room temperature

3-4 slices of pastured bacon

Steps:

The oven must be preheated up to 350 degrees before cooking.

Heat the coconut oil and sauté the onion, zucchini, and carrot and cauliflower rice in a skillet for about five minutes. Make sure to add the garlic at the very end and let it cool.

Mix the egg yolks in a large bowl, including the fresh parsley and the other herbs and spices. Add the meat and vegetables to the bowl and mix gently with your hands until just assimilated.

Transfer the mixture to a 9 x 5 loaf pan and make sure to spread the mixture evenly into the corners. Place the bacon strips across the top, fitting and tucking them in to the ends if they don't fit in the pan.

Cook for 45-50 minutes, or until the internal temperature reaches 155 degrees. Take it from oven and carefully pour out the liquid, reserving it to cook vegetables in later.

After that put the loaf back in the oven for ten minutes under the broiler to crisp up the bacon. Let it sit for ten minutes before slicing.

7. Desert Recipes

Gingersnap Cookies

What you need:

2 cups pitted dates, which should be soaked in hot water for 5minutes and after that drained

¼ cup of blackstrap molasses

1½ cups of arrowroot starch or flour

½ tablespoon of maple syrup

2 tablespoons of coconut oil or lard

1½ teaspoons of grated fresh ginger

1 teaspoon of cinnamon

⅛ Teaspoon of ground cloves

⅛ Teaspoon of sea salt

¼ cup of coconut sugar (optional)

Steps:

Your oven must be preheated to 325 degrees before cooking.

The arrowroot, strained dates, maple syrup, molasses, spices, coconut oil or lard and sea salt need to be combined and placed in a food processor. Mix everything mentioned in the food processor. Blend just until everything is just incorporated but make sure you will still have little spots of date and ginger.

Place the coconut sugar and put it in a plate and take a 1½ tablespoon of dough, then form it into a ball, and after that smash one side of it into the sugar. This will form a 2-inch, flat cookie. Place on a cookie sheet lined with parchment paper.

Bake for 20-25 minutes, until they darken in color and are slightly more browned on the bottom. It is important to cool it first before serving.

Final Words

So these are some of the recipes that you can enjoy in the comfort of your homes without the risk of too much cholesterol or sugar because all the ingredients used are natural, organic and not processed. There are a whole lot more of deserts, beverages, and most especially, main dishes that are AIP friendly.

Whoever said that being on a diet means you have to quit eating the food you enjoy? This type of diet actually lets you eat your favorite foods by just making sure it complies with the basic rule that it should be natural, mainly fruits and vegetables and were food that people in the Paleolithic age consumed.

This kind of diet will surely help in the cure of several, if not all, autoimmune diseases all over the country and the world. It just takes patience, vigilance and determination to stay on this kind of eating and avoid any processed food.

Our gut needs to be taken care of at all times because the lining of the stomach might get too thin with the toxic materials we take in and it that happens, our immune system will go haywire and attack our good cells. Nobody wants to have this kind of self-tissue attacking disease that might be passed on to the next generations if we don't start and join the AIP caravan.

Start taking care of yourself by prevention and practice this diet today. It might just need some getting used to but it promises a healthy and sound body and mind which is what we strive to achieve.

Thank You Page

I want to personally thank you for reading my book. I hope you found information in this book useful and I would be very grateful if you could leave your honest review about this book. I certainly want to thank you in advance for doing this.

www.ingramcontent.com/pod-product-compliance
Lightning Source LLC
LaVergne TN
LVHW021743060526
838200LV00052B/3433